The Mo[n]... and the Ladybird

by Jay Dale

illustrated by Anna Hancock

Here is a monkey.

3

Here is a giraffe.

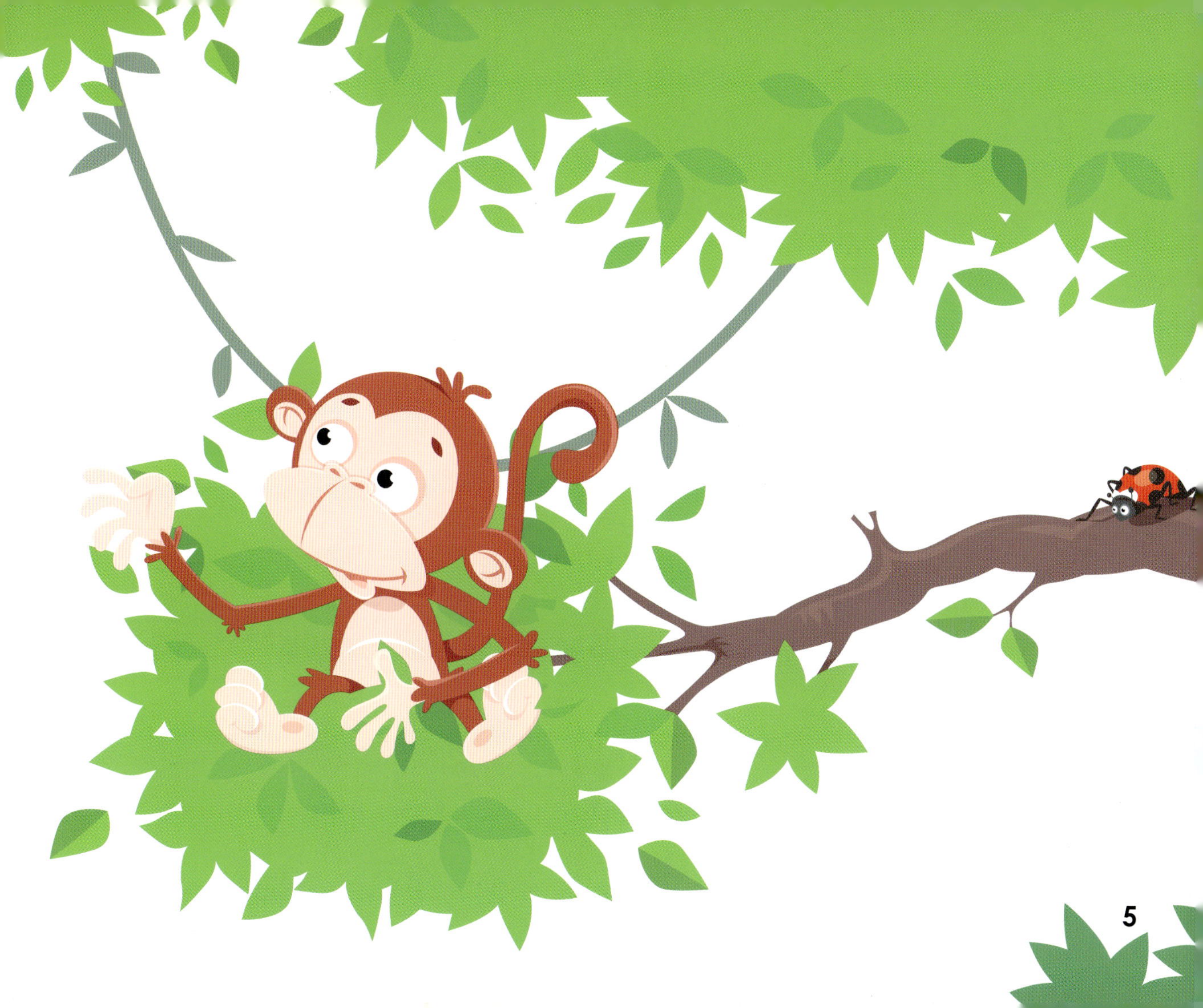

Here is a zebra.

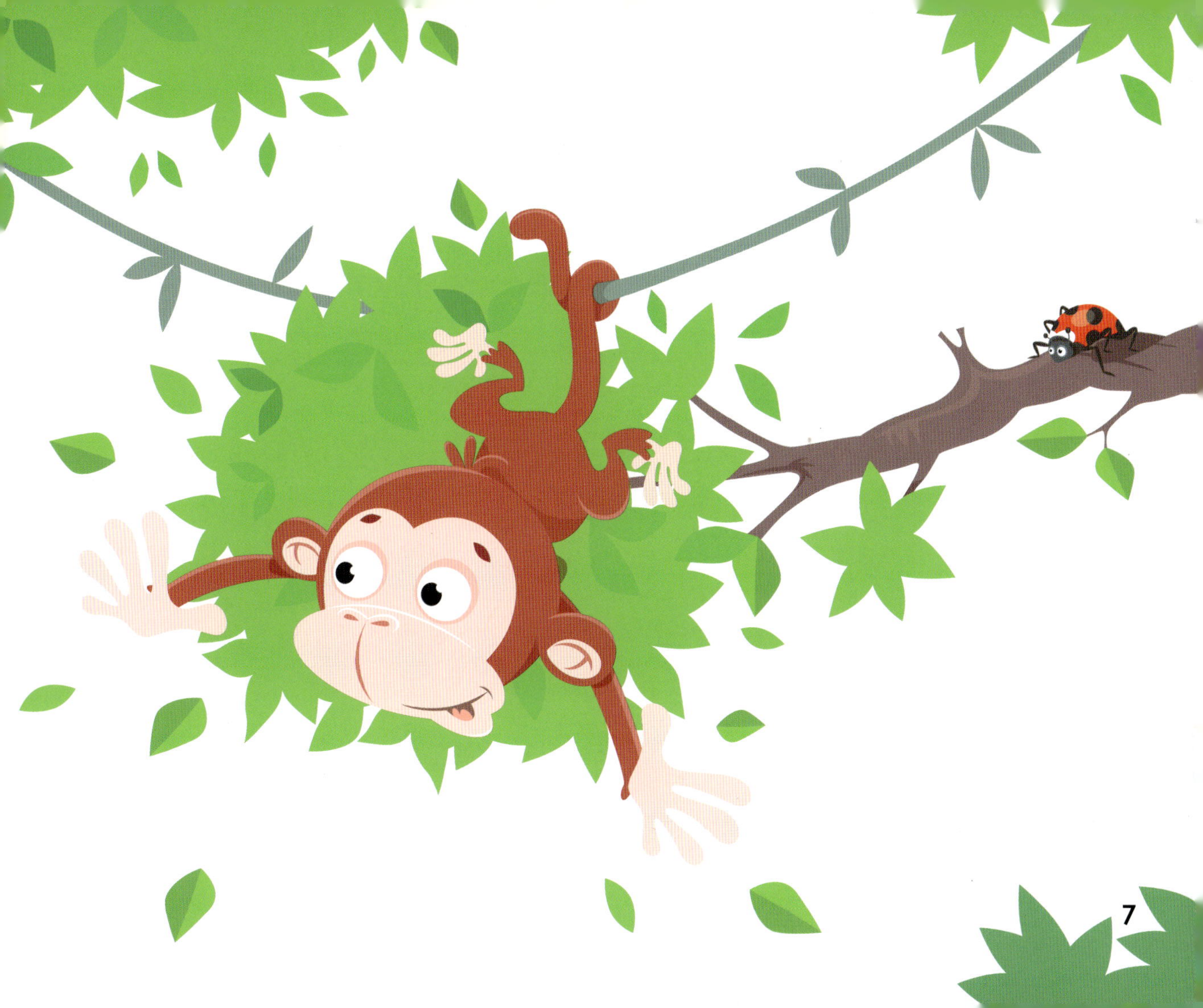

Here is a lion.

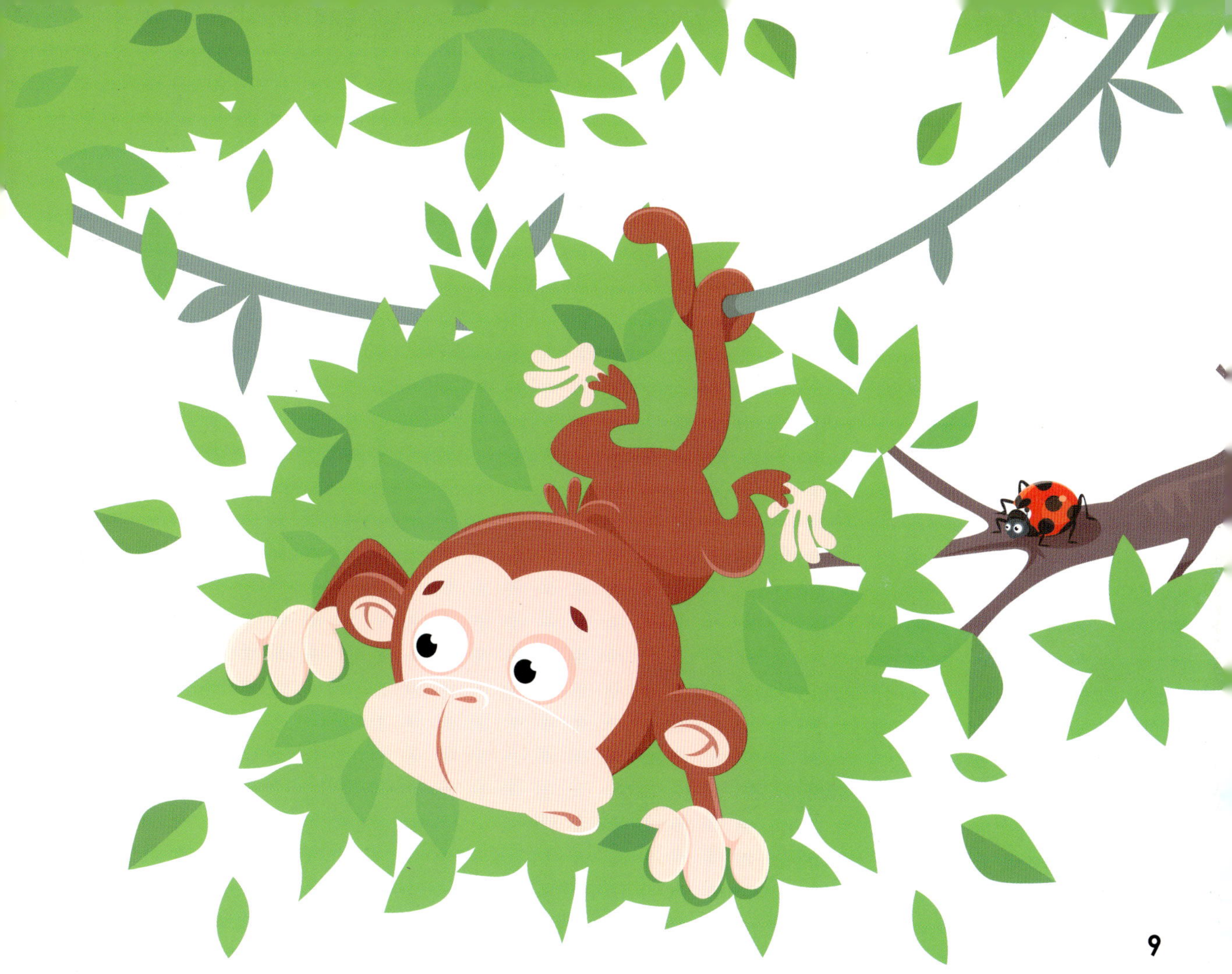

Here is a crocodile.

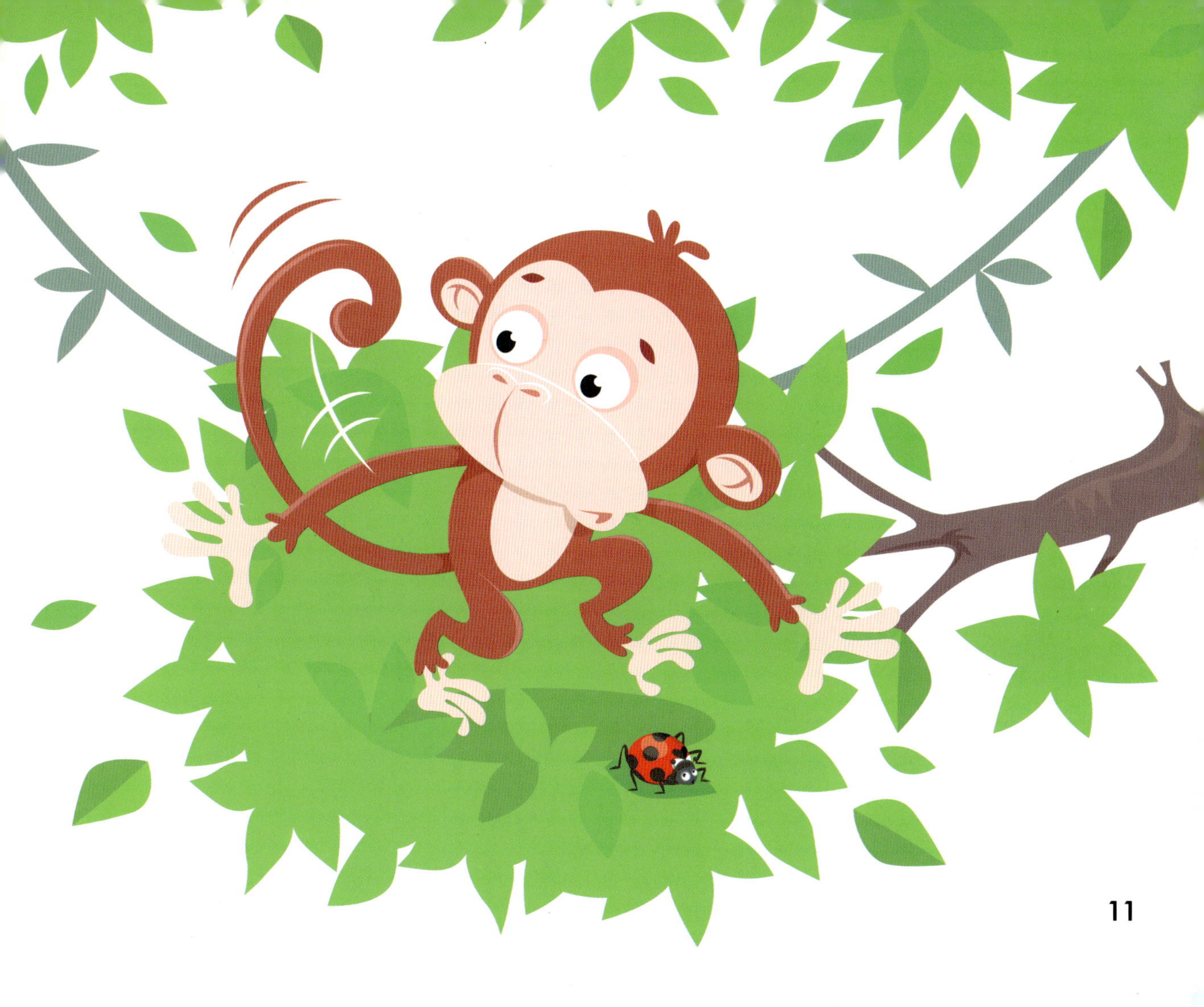

Here is a snake.

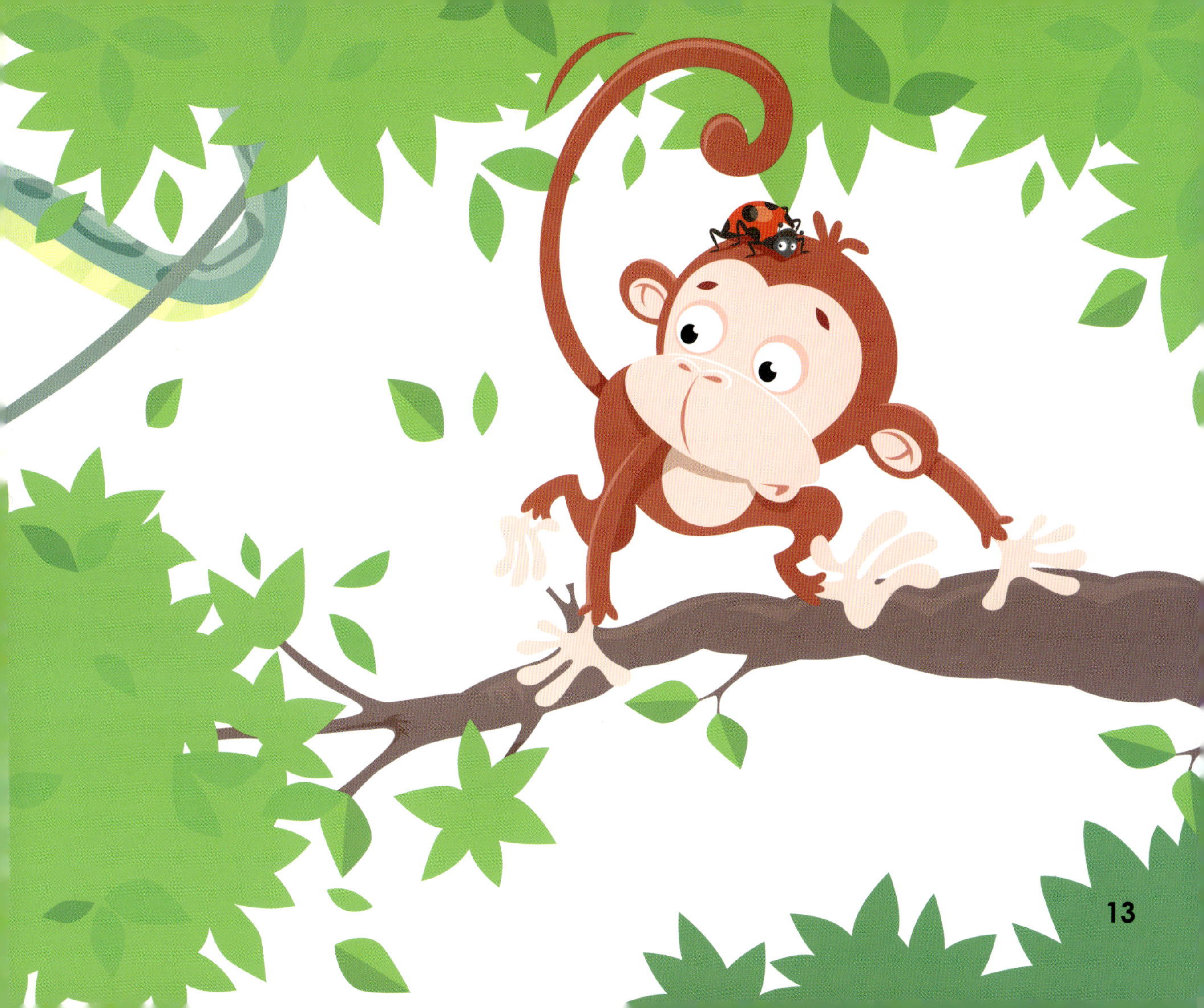

Here is a ladybird.

15

16